FATEHPUᴋ
SIKRI

DORLING KINDERSLEY
London, New York, Munich,
Melbourne and Delhi

Head of Publishing	Aparna Sharma
Art Director	Shefali Upadhyay
Design Manager	Arunesh Talapatra
Designers	Neerja Rawat,
	Ivy Roy
Editors	Dipali Singh,
	Suchismita Banerjee
Production Manager	Pankaj Sharma
DTP Designers	Jagtar Singh, Dheeraj Arora
	Harish Aggarwal
Photographer	Sanjay Austa

First published in India in 2008
by Dorling Kindersley (India) Pvt. Limited
in association with Penquin Book India (P) Ltd.,
11, Community Centre, Panchsheel Park, New Delhi - 110017
Copyright © 2008 Dorling Kindersley (India) Pvt. Limited

ISBN 978-0-14-306552-4

Printed and bound in
Gopsons Papers Ltd., Noida, India

Discover more at
www.dk.com

Discover more at
www.penguinbooksindia.com

FATEHPUR
SIKRI

City of Victory

A nondescript little village, Sikri's sole claim to fame was that it was the home of the Sufi mystic, Sheikh Salim Chishti. Then, in 1568, its fortunes changed dramatically. The Mughal emperor Akbar came to visit the saint. At that time, Akbar was at the peak of his glory – he had a powerful and stable empire, the royal treasury was comfortably full, and there was peace in the land. But Akbar himself was not at peace – his kingdom had no male heir. The anguished father went on a pilgrimage to the humble lodging of Salim Chishti, making one last desperate appeal for a son to inherit his empire. Akbar's prayers were answered. The saint prophesied that he would have three sons. On 30 August 1569, the first of these was born to Akbar's queen, Harkha. The grateful emperor named him Salim, after the Sufi saint, and decided to build a new imperial capital at Sikri as a tribute to the mystic. And so the rocky, barren ridge was transformed over the next few years into a magnificent citadel with a separate sacred complex specially constructed for the saint. From here Akbar marched out to conquer Gujarat and on his return, he renamed the city as Fatehpur (City of Victory). This was the first planned city of the Mughal empire and the monuments in sandstone exemplified Mughal architecture at its finest. But the splendour of this citadel was shortlived – it was abandoned in 1585, possibly due to shortage of water. Today, Fatehpur Sikri is a ghost town with palaces, mosques, and pavilions that offer a mere glimpse of their former grandeur – and a more sombre reminder of the hubris of kings.

⚜ **ROYAL CAPITAL**
Fatehpur Sikri lies 40km (25 miles) from Agra, Uttar Pradesh.

The Mughal Dynasty

One of the greatest medieval dynasties in the world, the Mughals established their rule in India after Zahiruddin Babur entered India from Central Asia in 1526. His descendants expanded and strengthened the empire. For more than a century afterwards, the splendour of the Mughal court was well-documented. In fact, the word "mogul", denoting a powerful personage, is derived from "Mughal". After the death of Aurangzeb, the last great Mughal, the empire declined. It came to an end when Bahadur Shah Zafar was dethroned by the British in 1857.

- 1526 **Babur** defeats Ibrahim Lodi and establishes the Mughal dynasty with **Agra** as the chief city.

- 1530 Babur dies, and his son **Humayun** accedes to the throne.

- 1556 Humayun dies, succeeded by his son **Akbar**.

- 1571 **Akbar moves his capital** from Agra to a newly built city near Sikri named **Fatehpur**.

- 1585 **Akbar transfers his capital** from Fatehpur Sikri to Lahore.

- 1605 Akbar dies, succeeded by his son **Jahangir**.

- 1627 Jahangir dies, war of succession follows. **Shah Jahan** accedes to the throne in 1628.

- 1658 Shah Jahan deposed by his son **Aurangzeb**. Shah Jahan dies in 1666.

- 1707 **Aurangzeb** dies and the **empire gradually declines**.

Akbar

Known as Akbar the Great, Jalaluddin Muhammad Akbar became emperor when he was only 13 years old after his father, Humayun, died. With the help of his guardian Bairam Khan, he extended control over northern India. After he came of age in 1560, Akbar achieved a series of military successes, his empire stretching from Kashmir in the

AKBAR THE GREAT

north and Afghanistan in the west to Bengal in the east and the Deccan in the south. His reign was marked by an efficient centralized government administered by *mansabdars* (warrior-aristocrats). He followed a policy of religious tolerance, reducing the influence of the *ulema* (Islamic scholars) and abolishing *jizya* (taxes imposed on non-Muslim residents), which helped to unify the empire.

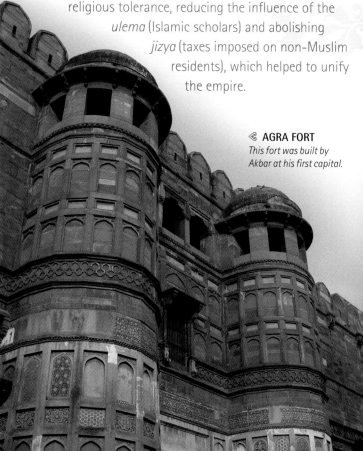

AGRA FORT
This fort was built by Akbar at his first capital.

Realizing an imperial vision

The vast stretches of India ruled over by Akbar witnessed the creation of impressive buildings like the palace forts at Agra, Allahabad, Ajmer, and Lahore (now in Pakistan), that symbolized his might as an empire-builder. Agra was his capital at first and it is here that he built the Agra Fort between 1565 and 1573. Forming a crescent along the Yamuna riverfront with imposing sandstone ramparts, it encompassed an enormous range of courtly buildings. Akbar then built a new capital called Fatehpur, a fine example of a Mughal city, constructed between 1571 and 1585. This capital was abandoned when Akbar went on to Lahore, where he had already demolished a 3000-year-old mud fort to build the Lahore Fort in 1566. He also designed and started the construction of his own tomb at Sikandra, near Agra.

⚜ COINS FROM AKBAR'S ERA
Gold coins were struck in Fatehpur Sikri, but the metal was refined in mints elsewhere in the empire.

♥ GRAND CAPITAL
Built atop a sandstone ridge, Fatehpur Sikri was planned as the magnificent new capital of Akbar, with superbly crafted buildings.

NINE GEMS

A connoisseur of fine arts, Akbar attracted the best talents to his court. Known as the *navratnas* or nine gems, this elite group comprised Abul Fazl, chronicler of Akbar's rule; his brother Faizi, poet; Tansen, classical singer and disciple of Swami Haridas; Birbal, minister

⚜ TANSEN
Dressed as a commoner, Akbar visits Swami Haridas at Vrindavan; Tansen is seated in the centre.

BIRBAL

and court jester; Raja Todar Mal, who overhauled the empire's revenue system; Raja Man Singh of Amber; Abdul Rahim Khan-i-Khan, poet, linguist, and general; and Mullah do Piaza and Fakir Azia-ud-din, advisors to the emperor.

COURTYARD OF THE DAULAT KHANA
Silhouetted against the sky are the graceful Panch Mahal and the Diwan-i-Khas, which overlook the Anoop Talao in the courtyard.

Sandstone Splendour

Stretching across the top of a ridge overlooking a now dried up lake, is Fatehpur Sikri, once the imperial capital of Akbar. It encompasses about 6km (3.7miles), with a high, battlemented wall running on three sides and the fourth opening out to the lake. It is from the highest terrace of Panch Mahal, the five-storeyed open pavilion at the centre, that a panoramic view of the palaces, pavilions, shrines, and gateways casts its spell on a visitor, conjuring up images of the days gone by. These architectural gems have been constructed in a fusion of Central Asian and Rajasthani styles, with intricate *jaalis* (filigreed stone screens), *chhajjas* (sloping eaves), *chhatris* (pavilions with umbrella-shaped domes), sumptuous carving, and surface ornamentation, such as those on spandrels (triangular spaces above an arch). The gateways include the Badshahi and Buland Darwazas that lead to the sacred complex.

⚜ **GRAND GATEWAY**
The Buland Darwaza is the greatest monumental structure created in Akbar's reign.

Entering Fatehpur Sikri

Standing sentinel, one after the other, a series of Darwazas (gateways) lead into Fatehpur Sikri. These gateways once formed effective barriers on the road to the royal complex. They included the Delhi, Lal (Red), Akbarabad or Agra, Suraj (Sun) or Bir, Chandar (Moon), and Gwalior Darwazas, as well as the Terha (Crooked), and Ajmeri Darwazas. The final gateway at the main entrance was the Naubat Khana (Drum House).

DOMED PAVILIONS

❦ **NAUBAT KHANA**
A roll of drums from this triple-arched gateway announced the emperor's entry.

chhajja

⚜ HATHI POL (ELEPHANT GATEWAY)
The remnants of two stone elephants flank this gateway leading to the harem palaces.

⚜ AGRA GATEWAY
The road from Agra enters through the pointed arches of this gateway to the royal complex of Fatehpur Sikri.

chhatri in Rajasthani style

TANSEN'S BARADARI

Gracing the eastern edge of the Fatehpur ridge, this single-storeyed, rectangular building called a *baradari* (pavilion) is named after the legendary musician, Mian Tansen.

⚜ PILLARED VERANDAH
The pillars of the verandah are crowned with ornate brackets.

STAR PATTERNS ⚜
The verandah walls bear inlay work in sandstone and marble.

Layout of the Fatehpur Sikri complex

Symbolizing an all-powerful monarchy, the Fatehpur Sikri complex is based on a large-scale, yet carefully envisaged plan. Approached from the dry bed of the lake, the Hiran Minar (Deer Tower) is visible, axially aligned to the Hathi Pol (Elephant Gateway). The rich array of buildings can roughly be divided into two parts – the imperial and the sacred complex. The former comprises the private quarters of the emperor, known as the Daulat Khana (Abode of Fortune), and includes the palaces of the queens. Here too are the halls for public and private audiences, and the treasuries. The Buland Darwaza (Lofty Gateway) leads to the sacred quadrangle, which includes Sheikh Salim Chishti's *dargah* (shrine and tomb).

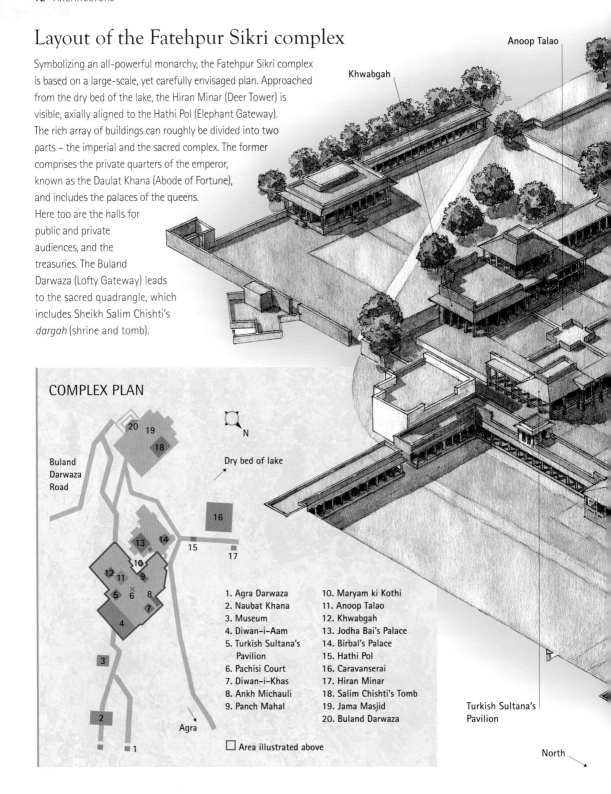

Anoop Talao

Khwabgah

Turkish Sultana's Pavilion

North

COMPLEX PLAN

N

Buland Darwaza Road

Dry bed of lake

Agra

1. Agra Darwaza
2. Naubat Khana
3. Museum
4. Diwan-i-Aam
5. Turkish Sultana's Pavilion
6. Pachisi Court
7. Diwan-i-Khas
8. Ankh Michauli
9. Panch Mahal
10. Maryam ki Kothi
11. Anoop Talao
12. Khwabgah
13. Jodha Bai's Palace
14. Birbal's Palace
15. Hathi Pol
16. Caravanserai
17. Hiran Minar
18. Salim Chishti's Tomb
19. Jama Masjid
20. Buland Darwaza

☐ Area illustrated above

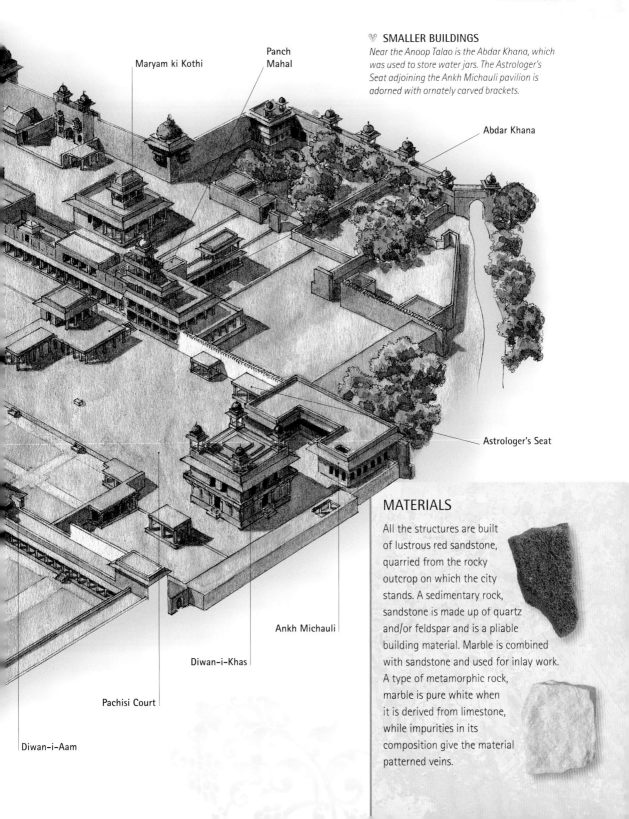

Maryam ki Kothi

Panch Mahal

❦ **SMALLER BUILDINGS**
Near the Anoop Talao is the Abdar Khana, which was used to store water jars. The Astrologer's Seat adjoining the Ankh Michauli pavilion is adorned with ornately carved brackets.

Abdar Khana

Astrologer's Seat

Ankh Michauli

Diwan-i-Khas

Pachisi Court

Diwan-i-Aam

MATERIALS

All the structures are built of lustrous red sandstone, quarried from the rocky outcrop on which the city stands. A sedimentary rock, sandstone is made up of quartz and/or feldspar and is a pliable building material. Marble is combined with sandstone and used for inlay work. A type of metamorphic rock, marble is pure white when it is derived from limestone, while impurities in its composition give the material patterned veins.

Diwan-i-Aam

Built along the sandstone ridge are the imperial buildings with three main areas – the official section, the *mardana* (men's quarters), and the *zenana* (women's quarters). Concentric terraces separate the public spaces, which include the Diwan-i-Aam (Hall for Public Audiences), Diwan-i-Khas (Hall for Private Audiences), and the Pachisi Court, from the Daulat Khana, the private royal quarters. The Hathi Pol (Elephant Gateway) leads to the spacious courtyard, surrounded by a colonnade of 111 bays, of the Diwan-i-Aam. Akbar sat in the hall every morning, three hours after sunrise, to dispense justice, and petitioners and courtiers gathered to listen to his address from the royal pavilion, which was draped with rich tapestries. The emperor's seat, on a carved platform within the central bay, is cordoned off by perforated screens. Opposite the pavilion, on the right of the path that leads to the courtyard, is a heavy stone ring embedded in the ground. It was perhaps used to tether the state elephant, which reportedly crushed the condemned to death.

⚜ PACHISI COURT
The court's paving is set in squares, like a giant chess-board, where Pachisi, a dice game, was played (pachisi means "twenty-fiver", the highest score at a throw).

✎ INTRICATE DESIGNS
Finely carved in geometrical patterns, sandstone screens line the sides of the emperor's platform; it was from here that he entered the Daulat Khana.

marble cupola

⚜ DIWAN-I-AAM
The pavilion is a graceful composition of a pitched stone roof, five arched openings, pillars crowned by ornate brackets, and chhajjas.

HALL FOR PRIVATE AUDIENCES

✺ ORNATE CAPITAL
The central axis of the hall is supported by a circular arrangement of 36 brackets that seem to branch out infinitely, the pattern inspired by the Gujarati style.

♥ CENTRAL PILLAR
platform where
Akbar's throne
was placed
The massive Lotus Throne pillar with carved brackets supported Akbar's throne on top.

Diwan-i-Khas

Blending different architectural styles, the Diwan-i-Khas (Hall for Private Audiences) stands in the northeast corner of the royal complex. Symbolic of the emperor's supreme power, Akbar's throne was placed on a circular platform resting on an imposing, richly carved pillar in the centre, while ministers and nobles were seated in the galleries radiating from it.

inverted lotus
on finial

DIN-I-ILAHI

Akbar also held private audiences for religious leaders and sages of all faiths, the venue being the Ibadat Khana (House of Worship), which no longer stands. He created a new faith called Din-i-Ilahi (Divine Faith) based on the teachings of various religions. In this miniature painting (right), he is shown holding discussions with religious leaders (Jesuit priests are in black) in the Ibadat Khana.

⚜ **STONE STRUTS**
Mythical makars or guardian beasts are carved on the struts supported by corbels (grooves) on the walls.

Ankh Michauli

It is said that the ladies of the harem played *ankh michauli* (blind man's buff) in this labyrinthine building, but its secret alcoves and deep wall recesses suggest that it may have been part of the imperial treasury.

⚜ **OPEN PAVILION**
Two halls are placed at right angles to the central connecting chamber in this thick-walled pavilion.

Anoop Talao

Northeast of the Diwan-i-Khas is the Anoop Talao (Peerless Pool) in the courtyard of the Daulat Khana. Serenely beautiful, this square water tank extends to 30m (98ft) on each side. Abul Fazl records that in April 1578, the emperor ordered the tank to be filled with gold, silver, and copper coins so that people could collect the "sublime bounty".

⚜ **TRANQUIL CENTRE**
A sandstone island, enclosed by an ornate balustrade, lies at the centre of the Anoop Talao, with four bridges leading to it.

Khwabgah

Within the Khwabgah (Chamber of Dreams) lie the private sleeping-quarters of the emperor, with an ingenious ventilating shaft. A secret room behind the Kitab Khana or library (that according to Abul Fazl housed 25,000 manuscripts), as well as the emperor's chamber, still bear traces of painted murals in yellow and blue that once covered the walls.

⚜ **ARCHED PASSAGE**
This covered corridor leads to the personal sleeping-chamber of the emperor.

Panch Mahal

This five-storeyed palace is also known as Badgir (Windcatcher) because its structure, with the storeys rising in decreasing sizes, is designed to cool the interiors. The building is remarkable for the varied designs of the columns, with motifs ranging from the *fleur-de-lis* (stylized flower) to the bell and chain. The ground floor contains 84 pillars, which incidentally, is an auspicious number for Hindus. The Panch Mahal is topped by a graceful *chhatri*, and was probably enclosed by perforated stone screens to veil the ladies of the court from public view.

☙ MOTIF VARIETY
Carved columns have unique designs such as the fleur-de-lis.

☙ LATTICE WORK
The fourth floor is surrounded by beautiful latticed balustrades.

☙ PILLARED SPLENDOUR
The second floor of the Panch Mahal has 56 pillars, with a row of six pillars in a north to south direction and another row of four pillars running east to west. The carved pillars differ in shape, some being octagonal, others circular.

chhatri

latticed balustrades

⚘ PALACE ENTRANCE
This double-storeyed doorway was guarded by eunuchs.

low, perforated stone railing

Jodha Bai's Palace

The most conspicuous building in the Harem Sara is Jodha Bai's Palace. It is conjectured that Jodha Bai was Akbar's Hindu queen, but he palace was actually the residence of several of the emperor's wives. Built in a fusion of Hindu and Islamic styles, it features graceful pavilions and enclosed balconies.

Harem Sara

A maze of interconnected buildings, the Harem Sara (Imperial Harem Complex) includes Jodha Bai's Palace, Panch Mahal, Maryam ki Kothi, and Hawa Mahal. The heart of the complex, where the high-ranking women lived, was screened to the east from the Daulat Khana. A vast pillared structure near the palaces may have been an enclosure for elephants, horses, or camels, but was probably used as servants' quarters.

❦ COLONNADED ENCLOSURE
The stone rings in the bays are said to have been used to tether animals.

Rajasthani-style *chhatri*

chhajja

❦ INNER COURTYARD
The palace consists of apartments linked by colonnaded corridors to an enormous, secluded courtyard.

Maryam ki Kothi

Probably the residence of Hamida Banu Begum, Akbar's mother (known as Maryam Makani, or "equal to Mary"), this two-storeyed *kothi* (house) was covered with frescoes, representing scenes from the Persian epic *Hamza Nama*, and gilt work, which is why it is also called the Sunehra Makan (Golden House). Stone eaves supported by heavy brackets encircle the palace, with carvings inspired by Hindu imagery from the *Ramayana*.

⚜ NATURAL LIGHT
Sunlight filtering through the delicately filigreed arch casts a glow on the interior.

Turkish Sultana's Pavilion

This pavilion overlooking the Anoop Talao may have been used by Akbar's Turkish queens. It is also known as "Superb Jewel Casket" for its intricately carved verandah pillars with arabesque designs. The brackets are decorated with bell-shaped, floral, and herringbone carvings and display fine filigree workmanship.

☙ STONE ROOF
filigreed
railing
The pavilion is topped with an unusual stone and imitation clay-tiled roof.

HERRINGBONE CARVINGS

Birbal's House

To the north of the harem complex is Birbal's House (a misnomer, since Birbal, Akbar's favourite minister, did not live here). It was probably occupied by Akbar's senior queens, Ruqayya Sultana Begum and Salima Sultana Begum, or by Birbal's daughter, who was one of his wives. A two-storeyed structure, it stands on a massive platform, with a pyramidal roof capping the porch. The interior is divided into three bays, separated by ornate pilasters that bear a variety of arabesque and floral designs.

✎ CUSPED NICHE
Rosettes adorn the spandrels above this cusped niche flanked by richly carved panels.

arabesque patterns on brackets

✎ LOFTY DOMES OF BIRBAL'S HOUSE
Rising from an octagonal base are two domes capped by finials on an inverted lotus base.

✎ FINE MOTIFS
This intricate design of lotus petals is bordered by geometric patterns.

ornate pillars

✎ BRACKETS
The brackets and pillars in the house are elaborately carved.

FLORAL PATTERNS

Sangin Burj

Unique for its monumental outer arch, which proclaims the might of its builder by its size, the Sangin Burj (Massive Bastion) is a structure that, together with the Hathi Pol, forms the grand gateway to the harem complex. Made of red and buff sandstone covered with semi-circular patterns, the Burj is in an octagonal form. Combined with its arches, the whole effect is one of strength blended with elegance.

POINTED ARCHES OF THE NAGINA MASJID

Nagina Masjid

A private mosque for the ladies of the imperial harem, the Nagina (or Jewel) Masjid stands at the north of the harem complex. Divided into three bays by square pillars, it has *mihrabs* (niches) ornamented with finely carved rosettes on the spandrels above the arches.

Hawa Mahal

To the right of Jodha Bai's palace is the Hawa Mahal, the Palace of Winds. A pavilion designed to catch the breeze, it is enclosed by square columns and exquisite stone screens that ensured privacy for the ladies of the harem. It overlooks a garden laid out in the *charbagh* (quadrilateral garden) style, divided by channels.

WATER SUPPLY

Down the road from the Hathi Pol is an octagonal platform with a deep *baoli* (step-well) at its centre. Huge windlasses beneath the platform were  turned by men all day and night to pump up water, which flowed through aqueducts to the palace *hammams* (Turkish baths). Seen below is part of the pulley system used to supply the Hakim's Hammam, probably the royal baths, with water.

stone pillars

HAKIM'S HAMMAM
Ropes and buckets were attached to stone pillars on the terrace of this hammam to pull up water.

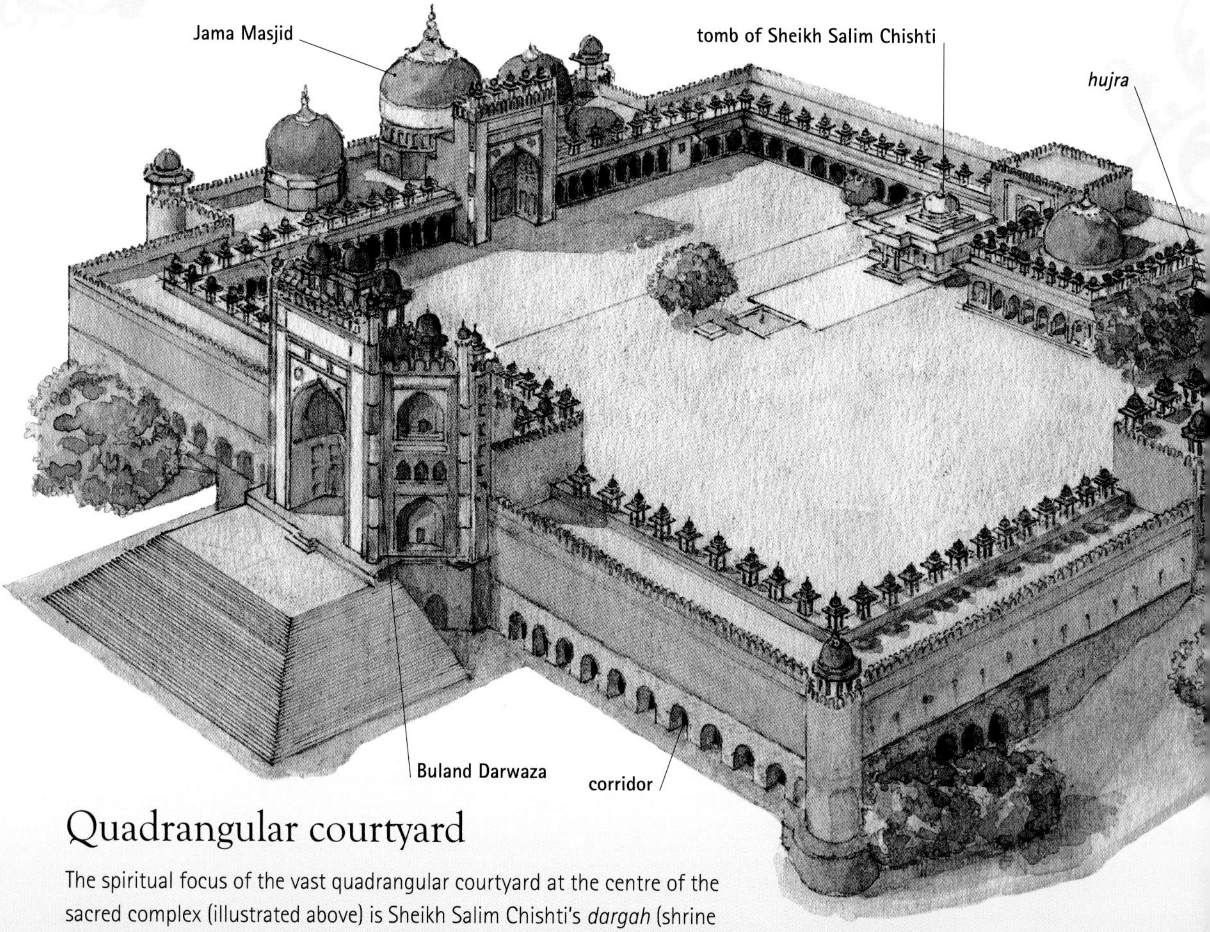

Jama Masjid

tomb of Sheikh Salim Chishti

hujra

Buland Darwaza

corridor

Quadrangular courtyard

The spiritual focus of the vast quadrangular courtyard at the centre of the sacred complex (illustrated above) is Sheikh Salim Chishti's *dargah* (shrine and tomb). The splendid Jama Masjid on the west, the Buland Darwaza (Lofty Gateway) on the south, and the Badshahi Darwaza (Royal Gateway) on the east border this enclosure. An extensive area measuring 110 x 130m (320 x 425ft), it served as a *namazgah* (open-air prayer place). The entire sacred complex was planned and constructed as a mark of reverence to the saint.

MONUMENTAL ENTRANCE ☙
The Jama Masjid is entered through this magnificent recessed central archway flanked by domes; each of the marble spandrels is ornamented by a single sandstone rosette.

Badshahi Darwaza

⚜ **ARCADED PRAYER HALLS**
Hujras *with flat-roofed pillared galleries run on the left and right of the courtyard of the mosque.*

Jama Masjid

A grand open mosque, the Jama Masjid towers over Fatehpur Sikri, situated as it is on a high point of the ridge on which the citadel is built. The congregational quadrangle is flanked by *hujras* (cloistered prayer halls). The mosque contains three chambers, capped by domes. The white central dome has floral patterns painted in deep blues and brown-red and the *mihrabs* (Mecca-facing prayer niches) are richly carved with inlaid geometrical designs, coloured tiles, and calligraphic inscriptions.

Badshahi Darwaza

It was from the steep steps of this Royal Gateway that Emperor Akbar entered the Jama Masjid to join congregational prayers. Adorned with bands of buff sandstone carved in geometrical designs, it has two arches, one above the other. From here, a view of the immense courtyard is overwhelming. The smaller entrance arch is cusped and decorated with stylized pomegranates, the tip of each arch ending in a carved lotus bud.

❦ **ARCHED OPENINGS**
Crowning the rows of rooms, built to accommodate mullahs (religious teachers), are a series of chhatris flanking the central archway.

Buland Darwaza

Erected by Akbar to mark his conquest over Gujarat in 1573, the 54m (177ft) Buland Darwaza (Lofty Gateway) dominates the sacred complex. It is reached by a great flight of 42 steps. The main arch of this magnificent gateway stands in the centre of three projecting sides of an octagon centred on the apex of the dome, and a row of *chhatris* crowns the parapet. The red spandrels are framed by bands of yellow-buff sandstone, below which are panels of marble inlay in geometric patterns.

SACRED VERSES
Calligraphic inscriptions from the Quran, cut in bold letters of the Naskh script, highlight the façade of the gateway.

WOODEN DOOR
Horseshoes cover the upper part of the door, hammered in by peasants for luck.

Salim Chishti's Tomb

The tomb of Sheikh Salim Chishti, the Sufi saint revered by Akbar, was originally made of sandstone and later sheathed in exquisitely carved white marble. The verandah of the domed cenotaph is enclosed by fine screens with chiselled hexagons and interlacing patterns. The cenotaph stands on a platform decorated with a mosaic of black and yellow marble, while stylized peacocks' tails adorn the bases of the porch columns. A richly carved doorway leads to the inner tomb that has a canopy delicately inlaid with mother-of-pearl.

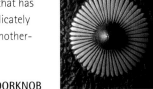

FLORAL DOORKNOB

❦ SERPENTINE BRACKETS
Carved out of a single marble block, each bracket in the porch is shaped into a graceful stylized snake.

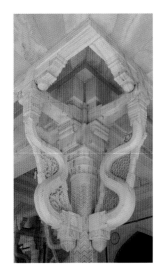

MAKING A WISH

Visitors tie cotton threads on the marble screen surrounding the tomb in the belief that any wish they make will come true, just as Akbar was blessed by the saint and had three sons.

Jamat Khana

Enclosed by an elegant stone screen and an arcaded verandah, this square structure was once an assembly hall for Salim Chishti's disciples and later, the tomb of his descendants. The doors have intricate relief carvings.

DOMED SPLENDOUR ✥
Rising above the sandstone roof is a grand dome surrounded by the cupolas of 36 small, graceful chhatris.

LIGHTING THE WAY
Lamps were probably suspended from the "tusks" to guide visitors by akash deep (heavenly light) at night.

Hiran Minar

Studded with stone projections resembling elephants' tusks, the Hiran Minar is believed to be a memorial to Akbar's favourite elephant. It is a 22m (73ft) high tower, with rosettes ornamenting the spandrels of the arched doorway. Bordered by a stone panel and flanked by blind arches, the door leads to 53 steps that wind up to the top of the tower. Here, a panoramic vista stretches before the viewer.

Stone Cutters' Mosque

The oldest place of worship at Fatehpur Sikri, the Stone Cutters' Mosque stands on the left of the Jama Masjid. Built in deep red sandstone by local quarrymen to honour Sheikh Salim Chishti, it shows slightly rough workmanship. Of the five bays, the central one has a richly cusped arch, where the saint would meditate, and behind it is an ornamented *mihrab*.

STYLIZED SNAKE BRACKETS

Caravanserai

Building shelters for travellers passing through was considered the moral duty of a Muslim ruler, and caravanserais number in the thousands in India. Standing as a fortified enclosure with octagonal bastions at its corners, the Fatehpur Sikri caravanserai is very well preserved. The quadrangle is divided by a low terrace, in front of which is a water tank.

SHELTERED ROOMS ⪢
Screened by arches, rectangular openings lead into rooms; each corner has three rooms arranged around a courtyard.

Rang Mahal

This palace, now dilapidated, was constructed in 1569, before Akbar decided to shift his capital to Sikri. It is said that Akbar built it for his favourite queen Harkha, the mother of Prince Salim, who was born here. The eastern gate's wide archway displays cusps emerging from the mouths of small elephants. In one of the courtyards is a pair of tall twelve-sided columns with remarkable double capitals, the beautiful brackets shaped like the heads of horses. Stylized peacocks' tails adorn other columns of the palace.

ARCHED NICHE ⪢
Rosettes decorate the spandrels of this red sandstone niche, the arch rising above the doorway.

⪡ **FLORAL BANDS**
Framing the recessed wall on three sides are ornamental bands with flower motifs.

Imperial city

Agra, the seat of the Mughal empire in the 16th and 17th centuries, is where it all began. It was in 1526 that Babur, a descendant of Timur, defeated Ibrahim Lodi and gradually gained control of northern India. He made Agra his chief city, and undertook several building projects, including a Persian-style garden at Dholpur, near Agra. Humayun, his son and successor, ruled from Delhi, but when Akbar ascended the throne, he chose Agra, strategically located on the banks of the river Yamuna and along the Grand Trunk Road, as his capital. The city flourished under Akbar, Jahangir, and Shah Jahan, attracting artisans from Persia and Central Asia, and from all parts of India, who built forts, palaces, mausoleums, and gardens, showing immense artistry. Agra became the political and cultural capital of the Mughal empire. With the decline of the Mughals, Agra was captured by the Jats, the Marathas, and finally the British.

⚜ DETAIL FROM THE TAJ MAHAL
These finely carved floral motifs on a marble panel show superb craftsmanship.

Around Fatehpur Sikri

Agra is the nearest city to Fatehpur Sikri, which is about 40km (25 miles) away by road. On your way to or back from Fatehpur Sikri, explore the historic city of Agra and its outskirts, with its unforgettable array of Mughal monuments. Two of these, the Taj Mahal and the Agra Fort, have been declared World Heritage Sites by UNESCO.

Agra Fort

Near the Taj Mahal stands the 16th-century Agra Fort. It encompassed the imperial city of the Mughal rulers and included palaces, such as the Jahangir Mahal, built by Akbar, and the Khas Mahal, built by Shah Jahan; audience halls, such as the Diwan-i-Aam (Hall for Public Audiences); and two beautiful mosques.

⚜ AGRA FORT
The ramparts of the fort form a crescent along the river Yamuna.

⚜ DIWAN-I-AAM
The emperor held public audiences in this colonnaded hall.

🔸 REFLECTED PERFECTION
Set in a charbagh *(quadrilateral garden), the Taj Mahal is mirrored in the water tank in front of it.*

Taj Mahal

Described as "a vision, a dream, a poem, a wonder", the Taj Mahal is renowned for its perfect proportions and exquisite craftmanship. Built by Mughal emperor Shah Jahan in memory of his favourite wife Mumtaz Mahal, who died in 1631, it is a sublime garden tomb, an image of the Islamic garden of paradise. Encased in marble, the mausoleum is crowned by a magnificent dome. It is flanked by four minarets, each capped by an open octagonal pavilion, that highlight the Taj Mahal's symmetry.

🔸 RED OFFSET BY PURE WHITE
The earthy red sandstone of the mosque adjacent to the Taj Mahal provides a fitting contrast to the pearl-like appearance of the main mausoleum.

Itmad-ud-Daulah's Tomb

About 4km (2.5 miles) from the Taj Mahal is the elegant tomb of Itmad-ud-Daulah, built by his daughter Nur Jahan, Jahangir's favourite wife. Described as a "jewel box in marble", the square, two-storeyed tomb is decorated with stone inlay, lattice work, and coloured mosaic work in arabesque and geometric patterns. It is crowned by a roof pavilion with two finials. The pavilion contains the replicas of the tombs of Itmad-ud-Daulah and his wife Asmat Begum, which lie in the chamber below.

DECORATED PINNACLES
At each corner of the tomb stands a graceful minaret, capped by lotus mouldings.

Sikandra

Akbar's grand mausoleum lies in the village of Sikandra, 8km (5 miles) northwest of Agra. As was the custom in his time, Akbar began the construction of his own tomb, but the actual monument was completed by his son Jahangir. The main gateway, Buland Darwaza, modelled on the famed victory gate at Fatehpur Sikri, has calligraphic inscriptions from the Quran. It leads to a walled garden where the majestic four-tiered tomb with its sandstone pavilions and marble-screened terrace stands. The grave itself is devoid of ornamentation, but the vaulted ceiling of the crypt is decorated with frescoes in blue and gold.

MARBLE INLAY
This detail of one of the panels on the Buland Darwaza shows fine inlay work in geometric designs. The large mosaic patterns in white marble on red sandstone give the gateway a richly ornamented look.

MONUMENTAL GATEWAY
A red sandstone structure with a colossal central arch, the main gateway is magnificent.

Tourist information

By Air: For international travellers, Delhi is the closest link to Agra. For flight options, contact the airlines or tour operators. **By Rail:** Agra is connected to most cities in India. The Taj Express and Shatabdi Express run daily services between Delhi and Agra. For enquiries, visit www. indianrail.gov.in. **By Road:** Agra is connected to nearby cities like Delhi (203km) and Jaipur (237km). For enquiries, visit www.up-tourism. com. **To get to Fatehpur Sikri:** Buses, luxury coaches, and taxis are available for hire from Agra. For enquiries, visit www.up-tourism.com.

Visitor's checklist

The best time to visit Fatehpur Sikri is between October and March. The complex is open to visitors from sunrise to sunset every day. Please check if photography is permitted in the monuments you visit. The entrance fee for citizens of India and SAARC countries is Rs 20 per head, and approximately US $6 or Rs 260 for visitors from other countries. There is no entry fee for children below 15 years. For updates on fees and timings, visit www.up-tourism.com.

Here are a few things you need to carry when travelling in India.

- Drinking water, torch, map or guidebook, mosquito repellent, sunblock
- First aid kit, medication for tropical diseases like diarrhoea, dysentery, and malaria, water purification tablets
- Light cotton clothes in summer, woollens in winter

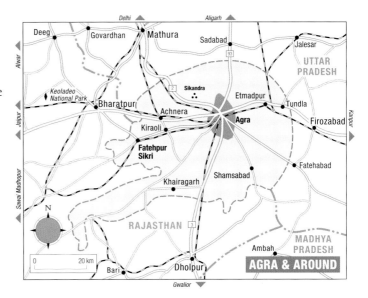

- Hat, umbrella or raincoat, easy-to-remove footwear
- Credit cards or traveller's cheques (optional, but advisable)
- Indian currency in denominations of Rs 1000, Rs 500, Rs 100, Rs 50, Rs 20, and Rs10
- Loose change in the form of 5, 2, and 1 rupee coins

Publisher's acknowledgements

Dorling Kindersley and Penguin Books India would like to thank the following people for their help and guidance in preparing this book:
Dr Narayani Gupta and Ranjana Sengupta for reviewing the text so painstakingly; Punita Singh, Manager, Rough Guides India, for getting us permission to use the maps in the book; Jayaprakash Mishra of Rough Guides India and Suresh Kumar of DK Travel Guides for helping us with the maps.

Abbreviations key: a=above, b=bottom, c=centre, f=far, l=left, t=top, r=right

Jacket Image: **Sanjay Austa**.

Notes